by Iain Gray

Lang**Syne**

PUBLISHING

WRITING *to* REMEMBER

LangSyne

PUBLISHING

WRITING *to* REMEMBER

Vineyard Business Centre,
Pathhead, Midlothian EH37 5XP
Tel: 01875 321 203 Fax: 01875 321 233
E-mail: info@lang-syne.co.uk
www.langsyneshop.co.uk

Design by Dorothy Meikle
Printed by Ricoh Print Scotland
© Lang Syne Publishers Ltd 2010

ISBN 978-1-85217-378-4

Watt

MOTTO:
By fidelity and confidence.

CREST:
A falcon, hooded and belled.

NAME variations include:
Wath
Wathes
Watts
Wattys
Watties
MacWatt
MacWattie

Echoes of a far distant past
can still be found in most names

Chapter one:

Origins of Scottish surnames

by George Forbes

It all began with the Normans.

For it was they who introduced surnames into common usage more than a thousand years ago, initially based on the title of their estates, local villages and chateaux in France to distinguish and identify these landholdings, usually acquired at the point of a bloodstained sword.

Such grand descriptions also helped enhance the prestige of these arrogant warlords and generally glorify their lofty positions high above the humble serfs slaving away below in the pecking order who only had single names, often with Biblical connotations as in Pierre and Jacques.

The only descriptive distinctions among this peasantry concerned their occupations, like Pierre the swineherd or Jacques the ferryman.

The Normans themselves were originally Vikings (or Northmen) who raided, colonised and eventually settled down around the French coastline.

They had sailed up the Seine in their longboats in 900 AD under their ferocious leader Rollo and ruled the roost in north east France before sailing over to conquer England, bringing their relatively new tradition of having surnames with them.

It took another hundred years for the Normans to percolate northwards and surnames did not begin to appear in Scotland until the thirteenth century.

These adventurous knights brought an aura of chivalry with them and it was said no damsel of any distinction would marry a man unless he had at least two names.

The family names included that of Scotland's great hero Robert De Brus and his compatriots were warriors from families like the De Morevils, De Umphravils, De Berkelais, De Quincis, De Viponts and De Vaux.

As the knights settled the boundaries of their vast estates, they took territorial names, as in Hamilton, Moray, Crawford, Cunningham, Dunbar, Ross, Wemyss, Dundas, Galloway, Renfrew, Greenhill, Hazelwood, Sandylands and Church-hill.

Other names, though not with any obvious geographical or topographical features, nevertheless derived from ancient parishes like Douglas, Forbes, Dalyell and Guthrie.

Other surnames were coined in connection with occupations, castles or legendary deeds. Stuart originated in the word steward, a prestigious post which was an integral part of any large medieval household. The same applied to Cooks, Chamberlains, Constables and Porters.

Borders towns and forts – needed in areas like the Debateable Lands which were constantly fought over by feuding local families – had their own distinctive names; and it was often from them that the resident groups took their communal titles, as in the Grahams of Annandale, the Elliots and Armstrongs of the East Marches, the Scotts and Kerrs of Teviotdale and Eskdale.

Even physical attributes crept into surnames, as in Small, Little and More (the latter being 'beg' in Gaelic), Long or Lang, Stark, Stout, Strong or Strang and even Jolly.

Mieklejohns would have had the strength of several men, while Littlejohn was named after the legendary sidekick of Robin Hood.

Colours got into the act with Black, White, Grey, Brown and Green (Red developed into Reid,

Ruddy or Ruddiman). Blue was rare and nobody ever wanted to be associated with yellow.

Pompous worthies took the name Wiseman, Goodman and Goodall.

Words intimating the sons of leading figures were soon affiliated into the language as in Johnson, Adamson, Richardson and Thomson, while the Norman equivalent of Fitz (from the French-Latin 'filius' meaning 'son') cropped up in Fitzmaurice and Fitzgerald.

The prefix 'Mac' was 'son of' in Gaelic and clans often originated with occupations – as in MacNab being sons of the Abbot, MacPherson and MacVicar being sons of the minister and MacIntosh being sons of the chief.

The church's influence could be found in the names Kirk, Clerk, Clarke, Bishop, Friar and Monk. Proctor came from a church official, Singer and Sangster from choristers, Gilchrist and Gillies from Christ's servant, Mitchell, Gilmory and Gilmour from servants of St Michael and Mary, Malcolm from a servant of Columba and Gillespie from a bishop's servant.

The rudimentary medical profession was represented by Barber (a trade which also once included dentistry and surgery) as well as Leech or Leitch.

Businessmen produced Merchants, Mercers, Monypennies, Chapmans, Sellers and Scales, while down at the old village watermill the names that cropped up included Miller, Walker and Fuller.

Other self explanatory trades included Coopers, Brands, Barkers, Tanners, Skinners, Brewsters and Brewers, Tailors, Saddlers, Wrights, Cartwrights, Smiths, Harpers, Joiners, Sawyers, Masons and Plumbers.

Even the scenery was utilised as in Craig, Moor, Hill, Glen, Wood and Forrest.

Rank, whether high or low, took its place with Laird, Barron, Knight, Tennant, Farmer, Husband, Granger, Grieve, Shepherd, Shearer and Fletcher.

The hunt and the chase supplied Hunter, Falconer, Fowler, Fox, Forrester, Archer and Spearman.

The renowned medieval historian Froissart, who eulogised about the romantic deeds of chivalry (and who condemned Scotland as being a poverty stricken wasteland), once sniffily dismissed the peasantry of his native France as the jacquerie (or the jacques-without-names) but it was these same humble folk who ended up overthrowing the arrogant aristocracy.

In the olden days, only the blueblooded knights of antiquity were entitled to full, proper names, both Christian and surnames, but with the passing of time and a more egalitarian, less feudal atmosphere, more respectful and worthy titles spread throughout the populace as a whole.

Echoes of a far distant past can still be found in most names and they can be borne with pride in commemoration of past generations who fought and toiled in some capacity or other to make our nation what it now is, for good or ill.

Chapter two:

On the field of battle

Although 'Watt', in common with 'Walters', is a diminutive of the personal name 'Walter', it is a distinct name in its own right with its own spelling variations.

It is a name with truly martial roots, with the originally Germanic name 'Walter' deriving from 'walt', indicating 'rule' and 'heri' indicating 'army.'

With 'Watt' a popular name from earliest times in Scotland, particularly in the northeast, it was also found in the form of 'MacWatt' and 'MacWattie', meaning 'son of Watt', long before it also came to Scotland in the form of those Anglo Normans who settled there in the early twelfth century.

A family of the name, descended from a famed soldier of fortune known as Simon Wathes, were also found from earliest times settled in the English county of Worcestershire, and while many bearers of the Watt name in Scotland appear to have led relatively peaceful lives – for example the merchants Alexander Watt, recorded in Angus in 1512 and Patrick Watt in Turriff in 1609 – others were not so fortunate.

This was through their kinship with the powerful clans of Forbes and Buchanan.

Recognised as septs, or sub-branches of these clans, bearers of the Watt name shared in not only their glorious fortunes but also their tragic misfortunes.

'Grace me guide' is the motto and a stag's head is the crest of Clan Forbes, who take their name from the lands of Forbes, in Aberdeenshire, which they acquired in the thirteenth century.

In addition to bearers of the Watt name, other clans that are considered septs of the Forbes include those of Bannerman, Boyce, Fordyce, MacWatt, Watson, Watters and Wattie.

It is along with clans that include those of Dewar, Gibson, Hammond, MacAusland, MacCormack, Morris, Watson and Weir that the Watts are recognised as a sept of Clan Buchanan.

This ancient clan, who trace a descent from Anselan O'Kyan, the son of an Ulster chieftain, have the motto of 'Brighter hence the honour' and crest of a hand holding a crown.

The O'Kyans took the Buchanan name from the lands of Buchanan, on the eastern shore of Loch Lomond, around Killearn, which were granted to them in the early years of the thirteenth century.

As kinsfolk of Clan Buchanan, the Watts were staunchly allied to the cause of the great warrior king Robert the Bruce during Scotland's bitter and bloody Wars of Independence – fighting for the cause at the battle of Bannockburn in June, 1314.

A 20,000-strong English army under Edward I's successor, Edward II, was defeated by a Scots army less than half this strength.

Scotland's independence had been secured, to the glory of Bruce and his loyal supporters such as the Watts, and at terrible cost to the English.

But Watts also frequently tasted the bitter fruits of defeat at the hands of their southern neighbour, most memorably at the battle of Flodden in September of 1513, when a contingent of Watts fighting under the banner of Patrick Buchanan, the eldest son of the Buchanan Chief, were among the 5,000 Scots killed.

The Scottish death toll also included James IV, an archbishop, two bishops, eleven earls, fifteen barons and 300 knights.

In a later and even bloodier conflict, Watts and the Chief of Clan Buchanan were among the 14,000 Scots killed at the battle of Pinkie.

Fought on September 10, 1547, near

Musselburgh, in East Lothian, a 25,000-strong English army under the Duke of Somerset decisively defeated a 35,000-strong Scots army under the Earl of Arran.

The battle had been fought during the 'Rough Wooing', an attempt by England's dynastically ambitious Henry VIII to force upon the Scots agreement for the future marriage of his infant son Edward to the infant Mary, Queen of Scots.

Despite their superior numbers, what led to the defeat of the Scots was that Somerset was backed by a fleet of naval guns at the mouth of the River Esk, and the early loss in the battle of the Scots cavalry after it launched a premature and wild charge on the massed and disciplined English ranks.

Bearers of the Watt name are also recorded as having been among those Scots who fought in the cause of their religious convictions.

A National Covenant, pledging defence of the Presbyterian religion, had been signed in the Greyfriars Kirkyard, in Edinburgh, in February of 1638.

Copies were circulated throughout Scotland, and the hundreds of ordinary men and women who subscribed to it became known as Covenanters.

Following the restoration to the throne of Charles II in 1660, the death knell of the Covenanting movement was sounded when a Recissory Act was passed, declaring the Covenant illegal.

Episcopal rule was foisted on the Scottish Church, and all ministers who refused to adhere to this new order were deprived of their parishes.

Along with their congregations, many ministers literally took to the hills, preaching at open-air meetings known as conventicles.

Lookouts were posted to keep a wary eye out for the approach of Government troops, and justice was executed on the spot for those unfortunate enough to fall into Government hands.

Constantly persecuted by the forces of authority, the Covenanters rose in futile rebellion in November of 1666 and, as a sign of the harsh treatment that was to be subsequently meted out to them, many of the prisoners taken were tortured and hanged.

Victory followed at the battle of Drumclog in June of 1679, only to be followed a few short weeks later by resounding defeat at the battle of Bothwell Brig, near Hamilton, by a force commanded by the Duke of Monmouth.

Nearly 800 Covenanters were killed and 1,400 taken prisoner.

Kept for several weeks in open cages in

Greyfriars Kirkyard, prisoners who agreed to sign a bond for future 'good behaviour' were released, but by November of 1679 more than 250 steadfastly recalcitrant prisoners still remained.

These included a Patrick Watt, from Kilmarnock, in the Covenanting heartland of Ayrshire.

The authorities decided to sell them as slaves on the steaming plantations of Barbados, and arrangements were accordingly made to transport them there aboard the *Crown of London*.

But the vessel foundered on December 10th off the headland of Scarva Taing, near the Mull Head of Deerness, in Orkney, during a violent storm, and an estimated 209 prisoners were drowned while still locked below decks.

Patrick Watt was one of the few who managed to survive and make good his escape, but his subsequent fate is unknown.

Another Covenanter who managed to flee his persecutors was John Watt, from the village of Eaglesham in present-day East Renfrewshire.

He had been attending a conventicle near the village when it was surprised by a body of soldiers.

All the Covenanters managed to escape, but not before Watt's long hair was pulled out by the roots on one side after a soldier grabbed it in a desperate bid to detain him.

He fled to Holland, only returning to his native land and village some seven years later in the wake of the Protestant 'Glorious Revolution' of 1688.

It is perhaps no surprise that his wife, believing him to have been dead for some years, fainted at the sight of him as he walked over the threshold of their humble cottage.

In a much later conflict, Joseph Watt was a Scottish recipient of the Victoria Cross (VC) the highest award for gallantry for British and Commonwealth forces.

Born in 1887 in Gardenstown, Banffshire, the fisherman had volunteered for service with the Royal Navy during the First World War, sailing in small drifters or trawlers to detect enemy ships and submarines.

It was while patrolling in the waters of the Otranto Strait in May of 1917 aboard the drifter *Gowanlea* that he and other drifter captains were attacked by an Austrian fleet.

Although his own vessel was severely damaged, Watt managed to rescue the seamen from other stricken vessels, and it was for this that he received the VC; he died in 1955.

Chapter three:

Inventors and scholars

In addition to the political and religious battles of their times, bearers of the Watt name have also participated in the more constructive pursuits of invention and scholarship.

Born in 1736 in the seaport of Greenock, on the Firth of Clyde, James Watt was the Scottish mechanical engineer and inventor who gave his name to an internationally recognised unit of power.

The son of a ship owner, Watt was somewhat of a child prodigy, showing a remarkable aptitude for mathematics.

Educated mainly at home by his mother before enrolling at Greenock Grammar School, like many Scots of his time he later took the long road south to London – in his case to study the art of making scientific instruments.

Aged nineteen when he returned to his native land, he attempted to set up business as an instrument maker in Glasgow, but the powerful Glasgow Guild of Hammermen blocked this because he had not served at least seven years as an apprentice.

Fortunately for posterity and the Industrial Revolution that was set to transform British manufacturing, Watt's skills came to the attention of three professors at Glasgow University – including the chemist and physicist James Black – who in 1758 installed him as an instrument maker for the university.

Later settling in Birmingham, and in collaboration with the wealthy entrepreneur Matthew Boulton, Watt revolutionised the development of the steam engine with his invention of the Watt Steam Engine.

Other inventions that flowed from his fertile brain included improvements to the oil lamp, a method of measuring distances by telescope, a device for copying letters and even a steam mangle.

He died in 1819, and is honoured through not only the unit of power recognised by the International System of Units as the Watt, but also through numerous statues and buildings throughout the length and breadth of the United Kingdom.

These include a statue in London's St Paul's Cathedral, one in Glasgow's George Square and one in Edinburgh's Princes Street, while the headquarters of Glasgow University's faculty of engineering is known in his honour as the James Watt Building.

He is also honoured through Heriot-Watt University, formerly known as the School of Arts in Edinburgh; named after the sixteenth century Scots financier George Heriot and Watt himself, it received its university charter in 1966.

Carrying on the Watt family tradition of inventiveness, it was one of James Watt's descendants who played a decisive role in securing Allied victory during the dark days of the Second World War.

This was Sir Robert Watson-Watt, the engineer and scientist credited as the inventor of radar.

Born in 1892 in Brechin, Angus, and after graduating with a degree in engineering in 1912 from what is now Dundee University, he later worked with the Meteorological Office before being appointed superintendent of a special Air Ministry research establishment.

It was through his work into radio telegraphy, as radar was then known, that before the outbreak of war he was able to design and install the chain of radar stations along the south and east coasts of England known as Chain Home and Chain Home Low.

These stations provided vital early warning of German bomber and fighter raids, and helped the Royal Air Force to win the Battle of Britain, bitterly fought over the skies of southeast England in the summer of 1940.

Knighted in 1942 for his contributions to the war effort, his book *Three Steps to Victory* was published in 1958.

Before his death in 1973, Watson-Watt was fond of ruefully recounting the tale of how, while driving in Canada several years after the war, he had been stopped for speeding by a policeman wielding a radar gun – a device, rather ironically, whose invention was based on his own pioneering work on radar.

In the world of botanical scholarship, Sir George Watt was the eminent Scottish physician and botanist who was born in Aberdeenshire in 1851 and who died in 1930.

Graduating from Glasgow University as a medical doctor, he later practised in India – but also found time to pursue his botanical interests, resulting in a ten-volume dictionary of all the commercial plants to be found on the vast sub continent.

Also from Aberdeenshire, Alexander Watt was the leading international botanist and plant ecologist who was born in 1892.

Graduating in agricultural science from Aberdeen University in 1913, he continued his research at Cambridge University, specialising in beech forest, before returning to Aberdeen as lecturer in forest botany and zoology.

Returning to Cambridge University in 1929 as its lecturer of forest botany, he also later held other prestigious posts that included visiting lecturer at the University of Colorado.

A prolific contributor to the *Journal of Ecology*, he was also highly influential in the development of the environmental movement of today, organising an international symposium in 1970 on nature conservation.

President of the British Ecological Society from 1946 to 1947 and a Fellow of the Royal Society, he died in 1985.

From botany and ecology to religious scholarship, William Montgomery-Watt, although a priest of the Scottish Episcopal Church, is recognised as having been one of the leading scholars of Islamic religion and culture.

Born in 1909 in Ceres, Fife, he became Emeritus Professor in Arabic and Islamic Studies at Edinburgh University, where he published a number of important works that include his 1953 *Muhammad at Mecca* and the 1956 *Muhammad at Medina*.

The first recipient of the British Society for Middle Eastern Studies Award for Outstanding Scholarship, and highly respected to this day by Muslim commentators as 'the last Orientalist', he died in 2006.

From Islamic studies to the often complex but no less interesting world of genealogy, honours, titles and heraldry, Robert Douglas Watt has the distinction of having served from 1988 to 2007 as the first Chief Herald of Canada, following the foundation of the Canadian Heraldic Authority.

Born in 1945 in Picton, Ontario, he had served for a number of years before his appointment as Chief Herald as an archivist for the Public Archives of Canada, while in 2008 he was appointed a Lieutenant of the Royal Victorian Order.

Chapter four:

On the world stage

Bearers of the Watt and Watts names have excelled, and continue to excel, in a diverse range of pursuits.

In contemporary music, **Ben Watt** is the musician and record producer who is best known as one of the members, along with vocalist Tracey Thorn, of the best-selling pop duo Everything but the Girl.

Born in 1962 in Barnes, London, he and Thorn formed the duo in 1982, going on to produce nine studio albums and, in 1995, the hit single *Missing*.

His autobiographical book *Patient*, a 2006 *Sunday Times* Book of the Year and a *New York Times* Notable Book of the Year, concerns his battle with a rare and life-threatening autoimmune disease.

In rock music, **Michael Watt** is the American bass guitarist, singer and songwriter who was born in 1957 in Portsmouth, Virginia, and is best known as a co-founder and member of the bands Minutemen and fIrehose.

Also in rock music, **Charlie Watts** is the

famed drummer, composer and record producer who has been a member of the Rolling Stones from its earliest days.

In addition to his musical interests, Watts, who was born in London in 1941, is also a horse breeder and accomplished commercial artist.

One of his musical contemporaries is the American jazz and rhythm and blues saxophonist **Ernie Watts**, born in 1945 in Norfolk, Virginia.

Best known for his collaboration with Charlie Haden's Quartet West, he has also toured with the Rolling Stones and features in the band's 1982 film *Let's Spend the Night Together*.

Also in jazz, **Jeff "Tain" Watts** is the drummer, born in 1960 in Pittsburgh, Pennsylvania, who has played with such jazz luminaries as Michael Brecker, Betty Carter and Wynton Marsalis.

Back to rock music, **Peter Overend Watts**, born in 1947 in Birmingham, is the record producer and bass guitarist who was a founding member of the British band Mott the Hoople.

In a wholly different musical genre, **Isaac Watts**, who was born in Southampton in 1674 and died in 1748, was the prolific hymn writer who is recognised today as a pioneer in the art of hymn writing.

From music to the highly competitive world of sport, **Jim Watt** is the former Scotish boxer who held the World Lightweight Champion title from 1979 until his final fight in the summer of 1981.

Born in Glasgow in 1948, Watt, who can boast 38 wins out of the 46 fights of his career, at the time of writing, pursues a career as a boxing commentator and analyst.

From the boxing ring to the Canadian national sport of ice hockey, **Tom Watt**, born in 1935 in Toronto, was assistant coach with the Calgary Flames when the team won the 1989 Stanley Cup, one of the most coveted annual awards in this sport.

Also a former coach and assistant general manager with the Vancouver Canucks, at the time of writing he is a professional scout for the Toronto Maple Leafs.

Still with ice hockey, **Mike Watt** is the former Canadian professional, born in 1976 in Seaforth, Ontario, who played for teams that include the Edmonton Oilers, New York Islanders and Lowell Lock Monsters.

In a different ice-related sport, **Nicole Watt** is the figure skater who was born in 1985 in Melfort, Saskatchewan.

The talented skier took the silver medal at

the 2001 Canadian Championships – despite suffering from the debilitating medical condition Juvenile Rheumatoid Arthritis.

On the pitches of European football, **Steven Watt** is the Scottish defender, born in Banff in 1985, who has played for teams that include Chelsea, Swansea City and Ross County, while **Sanchez Watt**, born in London in 1991, is the winger who, at the time of writing, plays for English club Arsenal.

On the athletics track, **Quincy Watts** is the former American runner, born in Detroit in 1970, who won two gold medals at the 1992 Olympics in Barcelona – for the 400-metres and the 4x400-metres relay – and gold at the 1993 Stuttgart World Championships in the 4x400-metres relay.

In baseball, **Eddie Watt**, born in 1941 in Lamoni, Iowa, is the former Major League pitcher who played for teams that include the Baltimore Orioles, from 1966-73, the Philadelphia Phillies in 1974 and the Chicago Cubs in 1975.

On two high-speed wheels, **David Watt**, born in 1978 in Townsville, Australia, is the international motorcycle speedway rider who won a bronze medal as a member of the Australian team at the 2007 Speedway World Cup.

Still on two wheels, and also in Australia, **Kathy Watt** is the racing cyclist, born in 1964, who won a gold medal in the road race and silver in the pursuit at the 1992 Olympics.

In the creative world of art, **George Frederic Watts** was the leading painter and sculptor of the Victorian era who became identified with the Symbolist Movement of his day.

Born in London in 1817, Watts, who was married for a time to the celebrated actress Ellen Terry before marrying the Scottish potter and designer Mary Fraser-Tytler, twice refused a baronetcy offered to him by Queen Victoria, but later accepted the honour of the Order of Merit.

Best known for his magnificent bronze statue *Physical Energy*, executed in 1902, he died two years later.

In the world of film and television, **Naomi Watts**, born in Kent in 1968, is the British-born Australian actress best known for her role in the television soap *Home and Away* and for roles in films that include the 2001 *Mulholland Drive*, the 2002 *The Ring* and, from 2003, *21 Grams*.

Best known for his role in the 1980s as the character Lofty Holloway in the BBC television soap

EastEnders, **Tom Watt**, born in 1956, is the English actor, radio producer, journalist and author who was the ghost-writer for English footballer David Beckham's best-selling autobiography *My Side*.

Also in the world of the written word, **Ian Watt**, born in 1917 in Windermere, in England's Lake District, was the literary historian and critic who, as a prisoner of the Japanese during the Second World War, was one of the men forced to work on the infamous 'Bridge over the River Kwai', in Thailand. He survived the ordeal to become a professor of English at Stanford University, while his influential *Rise of the Novel* was published in 1957; he died in 1999.

In the often cut-throat world of politics, **James Watt** was the Canadian politician, born in 1914 in Reston, Manitoba, who served as a Progressive Conservative member of the Legislative Assembly of Manitoba from 1959 to 1977; he died in 1985.

Serving as 24th Premier of Victoria from 1912 to 1913, **William Watt**, born in 1871 in Barfold, Victoria was the leading Australian Liberal politician who died in 1946.

Elevated to the peerage as **Baron Gibson-Watt** in 1979, James Gibson-Watt was the British Conservative politician who held government posts that included, from 1959 to 1961, Lord Commissioner of the Treasury and, from 1970 to 1974, Minister of State at the Welsh Office; he died in 2002.

In the fields of neurosurgery and psychiatry, **James Watts**, born in 1904 in Lynchburg, Virginia, was the leading American neurosurgeon who was a graduate of both the Virginia Military Institute and the University of Virginia School of Medicine.

Watts, who died in 1994, has the rather dubious distinction of having helped to pioneer, along with the neurologist and psychiatrist Walter Freeman, the controversial technique of 'psychosurgery', particularly the lobotomy.

One bearer of the Watt name with a particularly unusual claim to fame was George Darling Watt, better known as **George D. Watt**, the first convert to the Mormon faith to be baptised in the United Kingdom.

Born in Manchester in 1812, he moved to Preston as a young man, joining the Anglican Church Congregation of the Rev. James Fielding, whose brother Joseph had converted to Mormonism – also known as The Church of Jesus Christ of Latter-Day Saints – while in North America. Returning to Britain along with a number of Mormon missionaries, they were give permission by the Rev. Fielding to preach in his church.

Watt was among nine members of the congregation who were so impressed by what they heard that they decided to convert to the Mormon faith – the issue of who would actually be the first to be baptised being settled by them competing in a foot race, which Watt won.

Duly baptised on July 30, 1837, in the River Ribble, by the American missionary Heber C. Kimball, Watt later spent a period as a Mormon missionary in Scotland before he and his wife travelled to America to learn more of the faith.

A brief return to Britain followed, before the couple returned to America in 1850 to join the community of Mormons that had settled in the Salt Lake Valley, in Utah.

It was here that Watt not only worked as a reporter for the community's *Deseret News*, but also as a private clerk to the Mormon leader Brigham Young – also finding time to invent the Deseret Alphabet, a phonetic alphabet designed to assist non-English speaking converts to Mormonism to learn the language.

But Watt was controversially 'excommunicated' from the Church of Jesus Christ of Latter-day Saints twelve years before his death in 1881, for his adherence to interpretations of the faith deemed 'heretical.'